Forever Came Today
———————
Graham Lewis

Water Press and Media

Forever Came Today

Copyright © 2003 by Water Press and Media

All rights reserved

No part of this book may be reproduced or utilized in any form or by any means, electronic or mechanical, including photocopying, recording or by any information storage and retrieval system without permission in writing.

Inquiries should be addressed to:
Editors@WaterPressandMedia.com
or
Water Press and Media
3308 Ridgecrest Drive
Flower Mound, Texas
75022

First Edition December 2003

Cataloging-in-Publication Data
Lewis, Graham
Forever Came Today
80 pages
    1. American poetry
    2. American prose literature
    1. Lewis, Graham
    2. Forever Came Today
ISBN 0-9744524-2-4
Library of Congress Control Number 2003111054

Cover Art "One in Three" by Kit Morice
Cover design by Water Press and Media
Author Photo Bob Zordani

Printed in the United States of America

Acknowledgements

Many thanks are due to the editors of the following publications: *New Letters, New American Writing, The New York Quarterly, The William and Mary Review, The Laurel Review, The Chattahoochee Review, No Roses Review, Columbia Poetry Review, Colorado North Review, Zone 3, Farmer's Market, Rhino, Howling Dog, Amelia, Epiphany,* and *Gypsy Blood.* A few of these poems also appeared in *Voices In The Field,* a limited edition chapbook published in 1993 by Picadilly Press (Fayetteville, Arkansas).

I am grateful to the Illinois Arts Council for its financial assistance and am indebted to the Bread Loaf Writer's Conference for the scholarships that twice allowed me to learn from many great writers.

All my gratitude, as well, to my teachers and fellow students at Eastern Illinois University, Columbia College Chicago, and University of Arkansas.

About the Author

Graham Lewis was born in Trenton, New Jersey, and raised in New York City, Los Angeles, and Belleville, Illinois. He has earned degrees from Eastern Illinois University, Columbia College Chicago, and the University of Arkansas. He has won many prizes, including two Academy of American Poets' Prizes, The Kenneth Patchen Award, two Bread Loaf Writer's Conference Scholarships, an Ozarks Writer's Conference Fellowship, and a grant from the Illinois Arts Council. His poetry, fiction, cartoons and film criticism have appeared in many magazines and journals, including *The Quarterly, Asian Cult Cinema, New American Writing, New Letters,* and *The New York Quarterly.*

This book is dedicated to my grandparents, Robert and Elizabeth, my mother, Roberta, and my wife, Kathryn.

Table of Contents

Secret Lives

Brothers/5
The Bottle Tree/7
Illinois Dream/8
The Outlaw/9
Dragline/11
Christ Of The Ozarks/12
Tattoo/13
Blue Yodel #13/14
In False Point Tavern/15
Driving Through Kansas/16
Some Days You've Been Here Too Long/17
Bigfoot/18
Chanterelle, Bloodless Beneath The Leaves/19
War Paint/20
Two Ten-Line Variations/22
Cahokia Indian Burial Mounds, 1979/23
At The Gates of Dixie Trucker Heaven/24
That's For Sure, Pal/25
Candy/27
My Jesus Gonna Be Here/28
Swan/29
Johnny Ace/31
The Undertaker's Song/32
Apostle/33
Secret Life/35

Lester's Tales of the Seasons

Spring/39
Summer/40
Fall/41
Winter/42

Our Lady of the Fields

The Miracles of St. Marjorie/47
Marjorie Walks On Water/48
Marjorie In Season/49
Marjorie Among The Crows/50
The Baths of St. Marjorie/51
Marjorie In Exile/52

The Turner Sideshow, 1933

Baby/57
Toby The Half-Boy/58
The Talker's Eulogy for The Human Wart/59
The Midget Clown Brigade/60
Lady Seer and Mr. Slate/61
Serpentina Reconsiders/62

Forever Came Today

*They are destroyed
from morning to evening:
they perish forever
without any regarding it.*

Job 4:20

*Why am I the way I am?
Because those coffins
keep passing by me, man,
those coffins keep passing by.*

Jerry Lee Lewis

Secret Lives

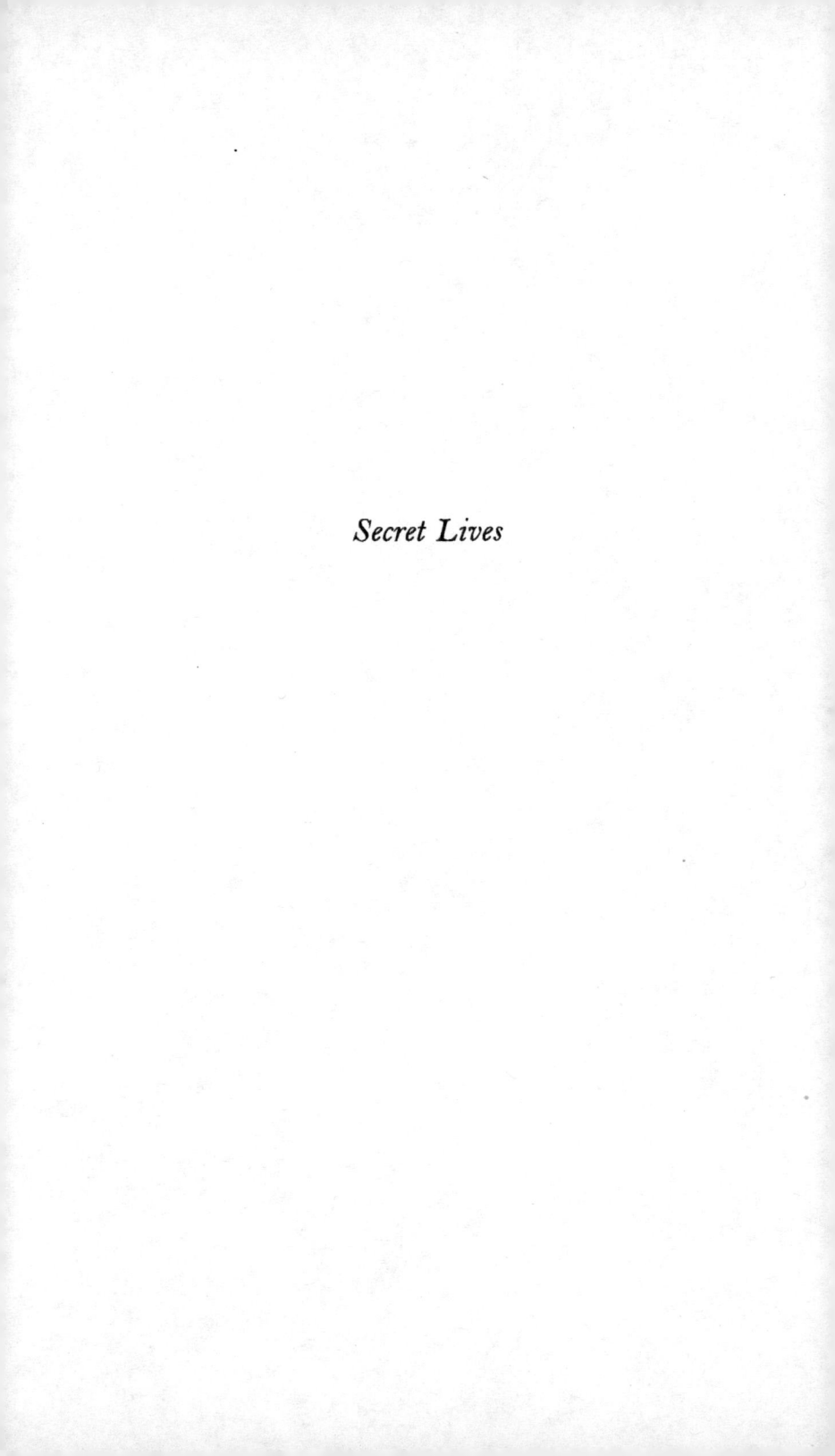

Brothers

When Joplin smiled, birds fell dead.

He took Daddy's rifle as always.
This time we saw a man on a horse
walking slow through the woods.
Watch, Joplin said.
One shot. The man went stiff,
pitched back and fell.
Joplin shouted at his bullseye.
The horse reared once and ran.

The man was alive, his jaw
working to catch air like a catfish.
The hole in his neck bubbled.
He held crumpled flowers in his fist.
Joplin swung Daddy's rifle
till nothing in the man moved,
till there was calm and a nice breeze.
Joplin's eyes were falling stars
leaving trails as he turned away.

We went through the pockets:
two dollars, a watch, a picture
of some woman leaning on a birdbath.
We kissed the picture, then burned it,
swearing that woman was ours.
I whistled a lick of Skip To My Lou.
Joplin hooted, kicking the man's legs
until I pushed him away.
He slapped me to my knees and spat.

We pulled the man into a wet ditch,
covered most of him with branches.
Joplin made me scoop mud for the rest.
I finished as the moon yawned
high up on its string in the dark.
Joplin cursed and howled, fired at it,
insulted its light couldn't be rifled out.
I squeezed a rock and waited,
his smile burning the back of my neck.

The Bottle Tree

Grandaddy stuck bottles
on broken branches for luck,
said bottles scared haints
because an empty vessel
could trap one forever inside.

One cold day Uncle Eudale shot
all the bottles from the tree.
They broke in pops
and a rain of colored glass.
Grandaddy yelled and cussed.

Eudale froze that winter, his face
black ice and tongue swollen
like a plug. Grandaddy said
the haints got 'Dale and it wouldn't
be long before they got us too.

I laughed at him. *There aint
nothin in them bottles but air.*
Grandaddy shook his head,
hung new bottles and prayed
at them with ancient rhymes.

Sometimes I'd wake early
to watch him. When he knelt
the tree seemed to glow, lightly,
like the butt-end of a night bug
or the moon through a church window.

Illinois Dream

We stand in the grass on a hill,
corn growing to the horizon
of factories, brick smokestacks
feeding black into a muddy red sunset.
Children skip rope on tar roads,
legs blistered, eyes milky and dim.
We laugh at desolate Main Streets,
post offices empty of letters.
I say my father fought in war,
killed men, for all this dirt.
The wind twists your hair
and travels on to the east.

There is no danger here, you say.
Only the fear of land so flat
time rolls pointless as tumbleweed.
Then it is dark, our lips touch.
Somewhere in the sky above us
bats whirl and scream, riding
their radar through night's
blind current. You point at the highway
below, a line of semi headlights
speeding away. A few bars
of Howlin' Wolf escape their rumble,
his growl shaping yet another tale
of how love alone survives its own death.

The Outlaw

That was the year of duststorms.
He came through the dead fields
Like the radio said.
Mama fed him beans
While Daddy hammered at his chains.
The numbers on his shirtpocket
Added up to thirty-one.

He stayed seven days,
Slept in the shed and taught me his knife.
It was sharp as lightning
And stuck in the porch like wood was butter.
Mama rocked and cackled,
Filling him jars of Daddy's best 'shine.
Mama said The Outlaw was righteous.

At night we listened to reports
Of troopers on the manhunt.
We laughed when they saw him in Rocktop,
Claimed he stole chickens in Starkville,
Found footprints by a saloon in Farley.
He and Daddy rolled smokes,
Small red stars glowing in the dark.

That last night we packed a satchel
Of jerky, water, and Grandaddy's Colt.
They were searching southwest
So he would head northeast.
The moon is too bright, I said.
It will see you and tell the law.
He smiled, passed me his knife, was gone.

Four days later the radio said
He was killed—ambushed
At a crossroad near Imperial, Kansas.
Daddy walked to town for a paper,
For the picture of troopers
Smiling down on The Outlaw's corpse.
Underneath, it read *Justice At Last.*
Mama cried into her sleeves.

Dragline

He brought the bucket of bass
with heads and scales and guts gone,
dumped them slowly into a bowl
of cornmeal on the table, said
Honey, they's ready!
She smiled, brushed a fall of hair
from her eyes and lifted
a black skillet from the wall.

Dragline rolled a scaling knife
between his hands while she cooked.
He saw the blade in her neck.
He saw the blood.
He saw her body beneath the porch.

When a spit of grease caught her
on the cheek, he jumped
to soothe it with his tongue.
They danced next to the stove,
tipping the skillet almost to the floor.

He kissed her neck sweetly while she cooked.

Christ Of The Ozarks

The beehive-haired lady in the gift shop says
this Christ, though sixty-seven feet tall,
is only half the god he was meant to be.
The builders ran out of money
and had to make do with a seven-story leg.
Still, tourists come to arch their backs,
shade their eyes and contemplate
the crude stone giant. Arms outstretched,
robe of a beggar, crow's nest for a halo,
he might be a pissed-off hobo
conjuring plague out of a boiling sky.
A child wearing a red cowboy hat
points his half-eaten chocolate bar and giggles.
His mother slaps his smeared face to tears.
Boy, it aint nice to laugh at Jesus she says.

Tattoo

FUCK THE WORLD it said.
FUCK THE WORLD on Jake's forehead.

That's some place for such a tattoo
Macky replied, rocking back
To drain our bottle of Old Crow.

Fuck the world Jake said,
Pointing at his forehead.

Blue Yodel #13

He hears snoring from another cell
—sputtering, stopping, starting—
his hangover stabbing him
where he moves. A spider
rappels lightly down his bare foot.
Just today (or was it?)
he was Eddie in his pickup:
whiskey in his lap, Haggard
on his radio, his shotgun clean
and loaded behind the seat.
He tries to sit up, to swat at
the spider. Nausea pulls him back.
The thought of whiskey belches
hot acid he must swallow or spit
on his pillow. He swallows
and cries, wondering where
his wife is, his mother.
At sunrise he'll holler
until somebody comes
to tell him what exactly he did.

       - for Larry Brown

In False Point Tavern

Arthur says he is trapped
by hooded strangers,
tied with wire, starved
inches from a pile of cold cuts
stacked neatly on a silver tray.
He wakes biting into his tongue.

Jacob believes
he hears a song over the corn,
a woman's voice lamenting
failed harvests long ago.
He says he wets the bed but never
can remember what scared him.

Mary talks long
about the man in her daddy's barn.
She slips off to him with the taste
of salt boiling in her mouth.
Mary wakes to fever, fingers
knotted tight around the bedpost.

I say my dream is blood
on the moon, on a golden knife,
on a white pillow in an empty room.
I wake slow, mapping its corners,
certain there is someone
I haven't slept long enough to see.

Driving Through Kansas

Cigarette clouds and highway diners.
A tornado of two-headed cows,
tractors, endless wheatfields
and homesick truckers
penned in for the night
with waitresses
named Wanda and Junebug.

I think of Lori Ransom, a girl
I knew at fifteen. She put my hand
on her breast in the Little League dugout
then said *I can't* and ran away,
leaving me with a hard-on
and twelve Louisville Sluggers.

Some Days You've Been Here Too Long

Rotten roads and droning
from the river,
mosquito clouds thick as dogs.
On Knob Hill, rusted grainbins
and the windmill
Tommy Dunne left behind
when he jumped off it last fall.

Over there, where shadows point
north of the radio tower,
the ruins of Becker's place.
They burned. All seven.
And half a mile east, June '95,
Don Wilkey held the Winchester
filling his father with buckshot.

You can't walk a street
without stories cruel as scripture
calling from every doorway:
Doc Lewton's girl a stripper in Dallas,
Latch Hogan's boy convicted in Joliet,
Charley Stone cruising for children,
your wife and Hank Frost behind the tavern.

Back at the house nothing works,
even your favorite chair sharp and mean.
You see a fast car on a flat road, miles
melting every breath. Someday
you'll find the place nobody here
knows, that secret town
where food is good and strangers
rejoice you've finally come home.

Bigfoot

Jackson Dean says *I saw it, by God,*
and I don't give a damn who believes me.
He brags that folks will believe a carcass.
They laugh and pound the table.
Jackson chews sugarnuts
from his fist square as a sledgehead.

His man Leo nods, neck on ballbearings.
Thass right, boys. We git its hairy ass.
Leo is a stooge with a gas can.
He might burn you out
just to watch his flames
do business with your barn.

But Jeffrey Lee says *Nossir.*
God made Bigfoot and whiskey,
pussy and poker too.
All God's things are good.
Jeffrey Lee gets five dollars
to show strangers his two-headed snake.

Big Bobby guzzles his whiskey.
I promised Li'l Bobby some nightfishin
he mumbles, his head dropping slowly
to the table. They laugh and clap,
chanting a rhyme of wine and whores.
Outside, something howls and closes in.

Chanterelle, Bloodless Beneath The Leaves

These mushrooms bleed nothing: meat dry
As beef jerky, skin rubber and orange

Without a mouth they are whole tongues
Shamelessly bathing in black bark and mud

For supper I'll eat their arrogance,
Shriveled and baked in cornbread stuffing

War Paint

Uncle, your hand trembled
as you brought coffee
to wake me
the morning of my first hunt.
You poured bourbon in it
though I just turned twelve.
Gets the motor moving, you said.
And don't tell your mother.
She'll eat my ass, hear?
I nodded and smiled, finally worthy
of the backpocket flask
you brought home from Vietnam.

Outside the cabin we checked
our Remingtons: safeties on,
barrels free of ice, shells loaded.
Then into the woods, both snug
in the orange caps Mother knit
to stuff our stockings last Christmas.

Before we made the stand
you held up your fist, the signal
to stop and wait. The brush ahead
rustled and grunted: a buck caught
by a tangle of branches, ten points
at least, steam jetting from its nostrils.
You pointed and I raised my rifle.
A sharp pop, a stumble and it dropped,
its lungs losing their last
against the rotten bark of a black stump.

For me, you dipped
your fingers in the wound,
painted warm stripes on my cheeks.
Like a little indian, you said.
I clapped and warwhooped
and danced a circle in the blood-spattered snow.

Two Ten-Line Variations (Concerning the Death of The Atomic Drive-In)

I

Today her stalls are silent, speakers long cut away,
screen snapped over jimson weed and gravel.
The yellow and red neon mushroom cloud is gone,
broken to dust, the lime green snack hut
a ghost of grease and cola. Once upon a time
this church rocked: Elvis, Juvenile Delinquents, Bikers,
Women In Prison, Giant Monsters, every Planet Of
    The Apes.
We came to worship, to drink beer, to fool with girls
or fight boys from other schools. They didn't believe
    like us.
They didn't comprehend the mystery, the grace, the
    revelation.

II

Last night I dreamed a Moonshine Movie Marathon,
Mustangs and Chargers, my hand on a bare breast,
a blue cooler glorious with beer.
I joined a brawl golden in sunset and trumpets.
We were skinny again, stoned, long hair and pimples,
bellbottoms and Black Sabbath t-shirts.
On the screen lovers loved, tommyguns rattled,
'shine-loaded hot rods flew over country roads.
The good got rich and the bad died hard.
Yes, it's true. I dreamed our lives perfect forever.

Cahokia Indian Burial Mounds, 1979

They must have thought something would save them:
a spirit in the river, a sacrifice, a certain star.
Whatever they thought, it never came.
They died, were buried, and disappeared.
Among them I felt treacherous and smug
because I was seventeen and drunk
and loved John Wayne in *The Searchers*.
Jonesy and I rolled Mexican grass,
guzzled Falstaff beer
and pissed our names into their sacred dirt.

They must have thought something would save them:
a dream, a dance, great mounds on a verdant plain.
Whatever they thought, it never came.
They died, were buried, and disappeared.
We drank and pissed and smoked there
till just before dawn,
stacking our beer cans into aluminum towers.
What else could we have said to their bones
to prove we were civilized, modern boys
born to sing our own songs of the dead?

At The Gates of Dixie Trucker Heaven

Even from the parking lot
I could see that the name
on the back of his belt was *Bear*.
I could see he was folded
over platters of eggs and ham
and grits and sausage
and biscuits and gravy
and homefries and pie.
He shoveled it all in, barely pausing
to chew, his fork flashing
like a garden tool in the neon haze.
He was not aware—or didn't care—
about the drool of bright yellow yolk
winding down the side of his cheek.

I pulled the door open and smiled,
profound animal hunger
possessing my weak eternal soul.

That's For Sure, Pal

A man come in the bar
and ordered a Schlitz.
I could smell his cologne,
that cheap shit they make
from the fat of cows.
Two-fifty, I told him.
I have a daughter, he said.
A pretty one for you.
Can you believe it?
I played deaf, served him
and went back to my regulars.
A girl come in a while later,
short dress nasty and tight.
Couldn't been more than fifteen.
Anyhow, he waved me over.
See my friend, he said.
Just as I told you...
you will like her very much.
He glanced at the door,
wiped sweat from his cheeks
with a purple handkerchief.
The girl nodded a mess of red hair.
With my thumb
I told them to get the hell out.
The girl narrowed her eyes,
snorted and spat in my face.
The man slapped her, hard.
I dove over the bar and pushed
them both out the door.

That night, in my dreams,
dogs scratched themselves blind,
the sky split then sewed itself
with lightning. I heard my mother
calling and calling my name.
I was young again, only handsome and rich.
But still all my lovers were Death.
It's a crazy fuckin world, aint it buddy?

Candy

The air is sweet with her sweat,
her perfume, her body and dance.
Her spectacular silicone breasts
roll and avalanche,
tumbling a supernatural gravity
inches from the tips of our noses.
Every man in this bar
would kill her, kill for her.
Instead our dollars buy a sniff,
a rub of calf, a promise for more
broken with the same smile
that swears it's true.
When she whirls and bends low
to reveal it all from behind,
the room drains to silence…
then detonates
into whistles, catcalls and cheers.
She winks at us through her legs,
welcoming the weakness, the want,
the desire of desire to love only itself.

My Jesus Gonna Be Here

He yelled that repeatedly from the corner
where pigeons roost and coo
from piles of uncollected garbage,
where yesterday a hooker in pink lingerie
beckoned crooked on a busted heel.
He yelled it between filthy
cupped hands, his coat collar
flipped high to hide his face.
His arms and legs shivered, summer
heat freezing him to the spot.
Trucks pounded through potholes.
The El screeched around a curve.
He yelled it and yelled it and yelled it
and stopped, tilting his head to listen.
Then he raised his hands to his face
and yelled it and yelled it some more.

Swan

From the entire city I chose her,
nameless, buying aspirin
at a corner drugstore.
She had the face, the brown
birthmark above her chin,
long hair black and unpinned.

I held the door open, smiled,
followed her to an ice-cream stand,
to the subway, then to St. Michael's
where she knelt at the rail
and touched her lips to wine.
All day I stood invisible
outside every place she knew.

No one saw me climb trashcans
in the alley, my fingers cut and numb.
The window finally gave, curtains parted
and her apartment glowed. I kissed
her ceramic eagle, rubbed my cheeks
against her bust of Beethoven,
shed my clothes and settled into her couch.

At sunrise I pushed her bedroom door
and entered on my toes.
Her eyes were closed but she lay awake,
the corners of her mouth trembling.
I fell forward. She screamed and trapped me
in a knot of thighs, hips thrusting
until everything inside us collapsed.

I slid broken from her bed, my knees
and elbows sore, my back shredded.
She wouldn't roll over to help.
She didn't like to speak.
As always before leaving, I placed
the white feather next to her head.

Johnny Ace (1929-1954)

I never thought
about pledging my love
to a bullet, but that's what I did.
The last thing I saw
were my brown eyes reflected
in the chrome of that .32 pistol.
Maybe I drank too much.
Maybe I was playing a game.
Maybe I was curious to see
just what would happen.
Rock and roll's a hard bitch
to please. One minute you nobody,
can't even get laid. The next
all of Memphis is after
you voice, you hands, you dick.
Then a day later you drunk
and nobody again. I never
found out why Fame pointed to me.
But I sure didn't want her
pointing away to somebody else.
Christmas Eve, 1954, Houston—
I gave myself the gift of forever.
25 forever. Hip forever.
Top of the charts forever and ever.

The Undertaker's Song

Speak to me of rooms you've slept in,
dreams of schoolboys, sports cars,
parties and promenades.
Whisper in my ear of the day
you slipped into death, your eyes
empty and loved ones aghast.
I want you grateful for my gift,
for the life I give back to you
as I braid your yellow hair,
paint red on your sullen lips.
Pretend you are mine, my song
devouring your silence. Kiss me.
Sing. Let your stiff tongue dance.

Apostle

I've preached and preached
until my throat burns, my hands
heavy bricks. Some nights
my poor feet bleed, cracked
from delivering Your Gospel.
Who but You could have seen
it would last this long, go this far?

Women fall in front of me,
naked of all things, begging
for my touch. Old men weep
at my smile. Even across
the forsaken desert they've heard
of You, Your Son. And they want
blessings, they want fish, they
want wine and dead men talking.

How can I, how can we deliver
those goods? As the soldiers
hammered the nails, teased Him
with water, smeared Him with shit,
I thought *Uh oh. This'll be it—
The End Of The World.*
Ha! Even that seems a long time ago.
Back when He was angry
and hungry and we feared
Your wrath behind His eyes.

Then He appeared to us dead
and Thomas had the gall
to poke his fingers in the holes.
I thought *My God, that can't be right.*
I was wrong then too.

Now there aren't enough of us
to lead these sinners home.
They are too many and too far gone.
When You killed Him, brought
Him back, then took Him again,
we suffered loneliness
no men have suffered before.

Sometimes still I feel Him hidden
in sand, in smoke, in water.
I look but see only my face.
I speak but hear only my words.
We pray the prayers He taught us to pray,
but we will never forget
how You Both used poor weak Judas.

We'll endure Your tests and games.
We'll tend Your labyrinth.
We'll write Your books for You.
We'll save and save and save
even if it kills every last one of them.
But remember this: they believe
You will one day make good on it all.

Secret Life

On full moon nights I am the storm,
lightning fingers cracking midnight's door.
I am the old barn, planks peeling, roof a mouth
open to rain and hail. Thunder is my song
of blood dried hard in dirt, black dirt dogs run,
black dirt cut by plow and combine, corn
burnt black by the sun. Lark and locust
know my name, their wings carving it in air,
in this cloud heavy and low. And I send
my hope in wind, heal you with a poultice of mud,
drown with you in the pond my heart leaves behind.
I follow as you walk the curves of this road.
Look for me in treestumps, catfish, cows mourning
their shadows in the heat. Look for me in the well,
the shed, the collapsed house on Signal Hill.
Look for me, love, in the secret life of all you see.

Lester's Tales of the Seasons

Spring

When Lefty Bowman
fumbled a board and sawed away
all his right hand fingers,
I kept the one they couldn't find.
It wore a ring and I left the ring on.
Sitting in Nodd Creek, Lefty's finger
between my knees, I waved
a hickory wand over it seven times.

At midnight I stood in a field,
held the finger in my cupped palms
and offered it to the full moon.
I made a hole in the ground; clouds
gathered and rolled above my head.
Rain began to fill the darkness.
Where I planted Lefty's finger,
a white flower curled from the dirt.

Summer

Mostly we sat and watched the road.
Chaingang Six from Camp Reed
drove by in trucks every dawn
and back again at dusk.
Our children spat, threw rocks,
danced crazy jigs and teased.
We let them, ignoring
the hateful stares of convicts.

Some nights, drunk soldiers
wandered into the yard.
In a line, arms locked around necks,
they'd stagger and fall as one:
a beast with many heads
crawling and singing and puking.
Maylee always tried to squash it
with a broom, sweep it back to town.

Fall

I found Henry Jordan in his barn.
He swung naked from the hayloft.
Behind the house he'd cut off the heads
of all his best hens, fixed a fire
for every stitch of clothes
his dead father left him.
Pinned through his right hand
a note said *Kiss My Ass You Sons A Bitches.*

The county paid his burial
and auctioned the farm piece by piece.
We bought Henry's bed for ten dollars,
hauled it home, used it a week.
Each night Maylee and I loved on it
she said she felt someone watching.
We pushed the bed into the yard, lit it,
cooked breakfast sausage over the flames.

Winter

I had to hurt Juke Hudson
when he started on me at the tavern.
I didn't want it, but he was too drunk
for any sense beyond a fist.
From the shadow of the back corner
he stuttered and ranted and insisted
that I had cheated him
out of Maylee, out of my own wife.

Then he ran and leapt. I put out
his eye with a beer bottle. No one moved
when Juke dropped and screamed.
Or when I kicked his head
until he was silent. I drug Juke
by his boots to the door, the icy rain outside.
When the sheriff asked around later,
nobody had seen a goddamn thing.

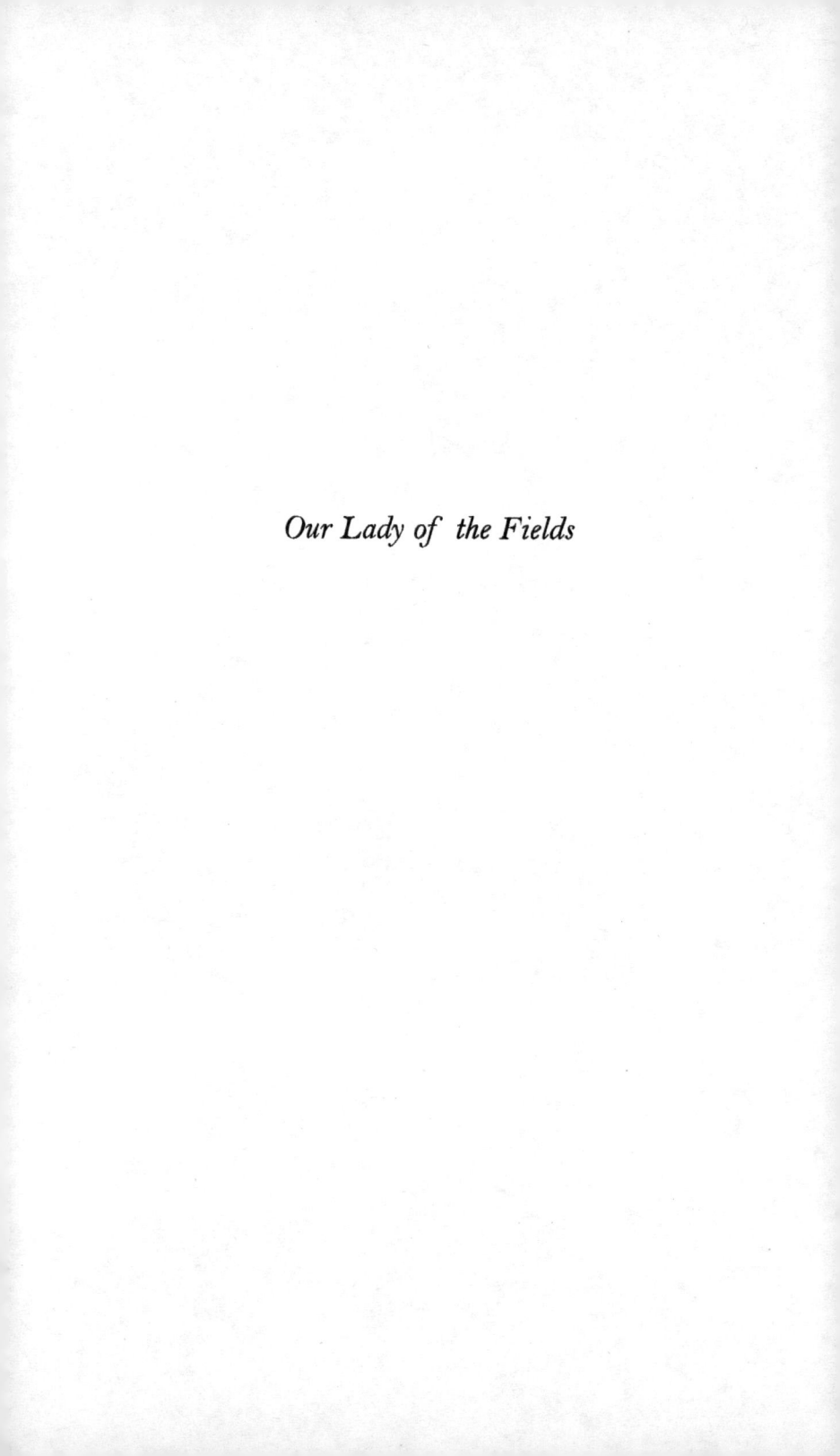

Our Lady of the Fields

The Miracles of St. Marjorie

Marjorie loves to watch crows caw
from the barn roof, fall to the rows
of corn, then lift and snap in a slow whip.
She'll smile, crawl among them to wait.
Sometimes the birds bring storms,
nails of rain shredding the fields.
Sometimes they bring taverns,
nights in trucks and fast loud cars.
Every sunday she rides
a drunken farmboy through sunrise.
Hidden in the furrows, Marjorie makes love
to the black wings blotting the sky,
her knuckles wet, fingers sliding easy,
consecrating the darkness between her thighs.

Marjorie Walks On Water

She sits talking to the crickets and rain,
the glow of town melting
to the flat black mud of Coles County.
This morning she heard music from the sky,
rolls of thunder teasing her into the fields.
She followed across gulleys and creeks,
each rumble a revelation just out of reach.
Hours later she found herself wet and alone.
When the moon came her breasts ached,
her monthly blood bitter and warm.
She sits rocking, rocking in the darkness,
telling it that always magical story
of how all she ever wanted
was to heal the sick and raise the dead.

Marjorie In Season

She feels the winter move in,
arranging itself around her.
Even as she watches
the landscape reassembles:
insects gone to husks,
leaves diving, animals buried
in snow. Then the ache, the
desire to undo everything
and push toward the sky like smoke.
She thinks she must tell him,
this new boy, tell him now to go
before she changes, finds herself
feathered and black. Already
she is on the barn roof. Already
her arms are in motion. Winged
and weightless she caws to the clouds.
The fields rise in welcome.

Marjorie Among the Crows

Marjorie draws in her coat against the cold
and thinks *It must be something else.*
Days have passed since the boy left, yet
she can still feel his hands and his tongue,
a drop of him burning her cheek.
He said he dreamed her at night, her hair
and mouth. She laughed, rolled away,
pressed her face into the pillow.
Thinking of him now makes him nothing,
a less than nothing she will again
cut loose like a withered arm.
Marjorie stands among the crows and cries,
their beauty useless in the evening light.

The Baths of St. Marjorie

Marjorie's eyes are bursting
but she will wear this night
Stars sharp tacks in hand
Gravity a breeze through hair

She is dying again
Fingers around throat
tongue plugging lips
cold bathwater breast-high
The clicking in her ears
says *Let go and breathe*

She won't listen
until the song is upon her
the flash in her brain
beautiful as a burning barn

Somewhere coyotes yowl
crickets fall silent
the sky rains ice
Somewhere the ground shakes
Men thunder to their knees

In Coles County Illinois
Marjorie inhales the moon

Marjorie in Exile

It's true river towns never make her happy.
All that filthy water, all those filthy people...
sometimes she wants to open her shirt,
press her breasts against a mirror
and melt into a puddle of foul levee mud.
Or write her ex-husbands love letters
saying she loved them more than cigarettes,
more than Tammy loved George, anything for a hoot.
This morning she woke to a vision: a parade
of Christs floating outside her motel window.
She wondered *Who does their laundry? Their hair?*
On a good day she might shake it off
and sing hymns to the pulse in her temples.
But today is not a good day. The river stinks,
she's on the move, and Jesus makes her crazy.

The Turner Sideshow, 1933

Baby

367 pounds
aint much
as fat ladies
go. Happy Ida
beats me by
over a hundred.
Some men grumble:
*Why, she aint
no bigger
than my wife.*
Sometimes
they want
their dimes back.
But other men,
usually skinny
and shaking,
want to meet me
later, to touch
me, my fat.
They want to
climb in it,
stick their thumbs
in it, own it.
They always
seem hurt
when morning
comes and I
send them
on their way.
I've had twenty
proposals
of marriage
and many, many
lovers. When I
get hungry, I eat.

Toby The Half-Boy

Beauty is the horror I breed
watching suckers clap and point
at my cartwheels, my climbing tricks,
my "Dance of The Legless Wonder."
I am in love with their eyes
as I trot at them on my hands,
fear and revulsion twisting
unspeakably perfect women.
I've got a leg for you, sister...
come and take a peek.

When we played Conway last year
I was so drunk I pulled it out
and let it swing loose.
I rubbed it on Serpentina's head
till the suckers tore the tent to escape.
Nights like that give me good dreams,
dreams of us strong and raw
and cruel, whole cities
swarming with us, and our children
rutting in the streets like dogs.

The Talker's Eulogy for The Human Wart

He was an ugly bastard. Even men
fell out of his way, studied the ground
and swallowed. Everyone wondered
how he stood the growing lesions,
the insult of each new wart.

He liked to say he was full of ice,
numb and hardly worth a bother.
But I heard him cry and beg for peace
when the ice turned fire and burned.
I'd bring him whiskey, gin, wine—

whatever I could find after the midway
darkened and the calliope stood dead.
Drunk, he'd laugh and tell me Jesus
had plans for freaks of this world.
Bullshit, I'd say. *Fairy tales.*
We argued that stuff for years.

I miss those nights, those talks,
his tiny eyes and giant voice
hammering at me. He often said
it was the pretty folks he pitied,
those who look in mirrors
and never see why they suffer.

The Midget Clown Brigade

We ran when the sideshow burnt:
me, Blinky, Major Domo, and Flip.
The flames brewed, children screamed
and all we did was run and hide.
By the time firemen came
a black stinking snow
swirled from the sky.
We watched them haul out the bodies.

Now we talk of marriage, kids,
yards with gazebos and swingsets.
We climb into our suits, our wigs,
our trick shoes and makeup.
We practice our somersaults and falls.
At night the wind stirs the woods
like crackles of fire, like laughter
we'll never make right again.

Lady Seer and Mr. Slate

Skinny man,

that writing on you
reads like heathen Chinee.
I love Mabel covered by
Hello Mama covered by
Happy Birthday Jake
covered by...

Arcane incantations snake
your sunken chest and back,
your beetle arms and legs.
But still that smile says
it don't hurt, never did,

never will. You wave
your shiny awl and brag:
Dig deep, write on my skin.
I'm smooth as a tit tomorrow!

The fools paying to mark you
have no idea what you are,
what you done.

I know.

I know that you took her,
your own baby sister.
You left her crying and bleeding
by a creek in Heber Springs.

I know it was cold,
that the leaves you shoved
her into were orange,
that the moon was full
and the boy you made is five.

I knew it all the first time
I touched you, raked my fingers
through your hair. You don't believe
a touch is all I need to read you,
but in every kiss you were slapping
her face, pushing her down,
holding back her screams
with your hand. Every nice word
you said to me had *I'll kill you
if you tell* behind it. She never told.

I didn't mind it much. I've seen worse
hid back in the minds of men.
But you should've been good to me,
you should've kept your mouth shut.

The carnies point and chuckle
every morning on the midway.
The clowns make suck noises
with their lips. Even the damn
townies been asking
how much I charge for head.

You don't bleed, I give you that.
Even where the awl opens you wide,
not a drop. But I know your secret.
I know how to make you holler and gush.
I know the right words to whisper
and just the right spot to carve them.

Serpentina Reconsiders

I

My mother believed I was punishment,
each scale on my torso a coin
men gave her for love.
That I had no thighs to shut tight,
no arms to push and slap with,
that I grew to have an angel's face,
brown hair and eyes, breasts
meant *men will want you,*
will put themselves inside you

and Mother was right.

For my thirteenth birthday
Stepdaddy Paul crawled on my back,
dug his tongue in my ear and told me
he had never been so hard,
had never seen a freak so pretty.
I screamed until Mother came
and beat his ass with a broomhandle.

They cried and prayed for days,
begging God for an answer.
When the answer came, it said
I held power no man could resist—
I was a snake and I was a woman and both
together had ruined the world. Thirty days
later, they sold me for five hundred dollars.

II

Twelve years I held the sideshow's
biggest draw, folks paying
fifty cents extra to see me in my den
of paper trees and grass.
Joe Turner loved me every night
then sold me to sheriffs, mayors,
rich men from the towns we played.
Joe was handsome and I loved him back.
Do your job, Tina. I'll make you rich.
I always did and I always got my cut:
a new Victrola, fine hats, books,
cases of makeup—it was a good deal.

It all ended in fire. Four men, wild
they lost at the midway games
burned us out with two bottles of hooch.
The tents went first, flapping sparks
on our wagons. Baby Martha, Toby,
The Human Wart, Lady Seer—all and more dead.
Joe pulled me from my bed and carried me
to a patch of soft weeds. He kissed me and cried.

We're done, Tina. We're all done now.

I lay there and watched the flames,
the pictures inside the flames. I saw myself
slither off to the woods, my breasts and belly
like water over rock and stump.
I tasted the mouse I ate whole, its body
writhing, kicking on my fangs and in my throat.
I felt the moon warm the scales on my back,
smelled rain on the tines of my tongue.

When the fires died, all I had left was ash

III

I want what the snake wants,
love nothing
the way the snake loves nothing.
I listen for the voices of night
calling me away. Circus after circus,
show after show, I shed myself dry.
Joe Turner married years ago.

I dream humans bent, brought down
by poison, love that sickens and rots them
from the inside out. I cut
through their guts like a spear.

Cold. Always cold. I can't
work when it's cold
and don't care anymore.
Joe Turner married years ago.

Round, white, perfect sins—
the eggs I lay
whisper and glow.

Book design and composition by Water Press and Media, using Adobe PageMaker 7.0. The text typeface is Bell Semibold, and the display face is Bell Italic. Bell, which was cut by Richard Austin for John Bell's type foundry in 1788, is considered to be the first English modern type. Bell was revived for hot-metal type setting by the English Monotype company in 1932, and was later expanded into a three-weight digital type family.

Water Press and Media - WP&M